More Water than Words

poems by

Kathleen McCoy

Finishing Line Press
Georgetown, Kentucky

More Water than Words

Place me like a seal over your heart,
like a seal on your arm;
for love is as strong as death . . . .
Many waters cannot quench love;
rivers cannot wash it away.

—Song of Songs 8:6-7

ACKNOWLEDGMENTS

"Through a Glass, Darkly" was published on the Tupelo Press *30/30 Project* web site in
July 2015. "Midsummer Grief" was also published in a previous version as a *30/30 Project*
poem.

"Green and Burning Oak, *Dair Glas Agus a Dhó*" was published in slightly different form
in *Green and Burning, Glas Agus a Dhó*, Word Tech Communications, 2016.

"Sitting Shiva in a Baptist Pew" was published in slightly different form in *The Crazy Child
Scribbler*, October 2015, on the Tupelo Press *30/30 Project* web site in July 2015, and in
Green and Burning, Glas Agus a Dhó, 2016.

"Hy-Brasil" was published in previous versions on the Tupelo Press *30/30 Project* web site
in July 2015, on the English Division Blog for SUNY Adirondack at blogs.sunyacc.edu/
division/english, and on *The Real McCoy: A Take on Poetry*, kathleenmccoy.wordpress.
com.

Publisher: Leah Maines

Editor: Christen Kincaid

Cover Art: Kathleen McCoy

Author Photo: Erin Reid Coker

Cover Design: Elizabeth Maines McCleavy

Printed in the USA on acid-free paper.
Order online: www.finishinglinepress.com
          also available on amazon.com

Author inquiries and mail orders:
Finishing Line Press
P. O. Box 1626
Georgetown, Kentucky 40324
U. S. A.

Table of Contents

Through a Glass, Darkly

The rafter-nested sparrow once again
interrupts my absorption in scrubbing honey
and marinara from bowl and fork as she hunts,
each feather twitching, fret reserved

for humans near her brood. Her head, feet,
wings rise, fanning an inconstant-eternal wind—
what Segovia's play of fret and string is to the tone-deaf waif
or pi to the pointlessness of random numbers.

She opens her beak of bounty—emanations of luscious
worm tumble into crimson caverns of desire.
I herd the cats away from the window.

Our sacred spaces, separate by nature, hover,
recognize *mysterium tremendum*
through shadows on the glass.

Oakroot

You clasp your loam close-by, snare
smiles as owls elicit surprise. Your stout
heart, overgrown from too much

care, your sanguine cheeks, oakroot fingers
reach into my chest, extend through my trunk
and down my limbs, grasp this pen and circle,

scribble, write, time no matter, no
ground for your roots. Your eyes
flicker, blue-ink wells one hour, the next

cauldrons full of the kind of fire
that curls around dead wood
to incubate the seeds of pinecones

or to console, cajole, instruct, amuse,
clapping applause or thunder.

Textures

In all its textures, rose-gold light
beams from your stained glass.

Never still, you
hum like sunlit water.

At your bottomless well
you never met a stranger.

Woman of water on a field of light, you
weave a nest of feather, moss, bone,

invite us in. We draw near you
as leaves turn up for rain.

Posies

As I enter the chill of the closed-off room,
steaming tea in cup—despite the silence,
in it, as it—you permeate the molecules of space,

words steeped in Chantilly and Earl Grey.
Wisdom wields its weight in memory, in each
glance and gesture of a stark, supple hand.

Part of me has melted into the ocean
to swim with you who swim for the first time
with all the dashing horses.

You and we form a trinity chanting
"Ring Around the Rosie." *Fingers of melting
ice write these words. A-tisket. A-tasket.*

Do you hear that ringing, meaning—what?
Mama, don't stop singing. Everything
and nothing and everything again.

*Oh, sweet Jesus, we claw at your hem for just
one touch. One touch.* Can you see the glory?
Magnolias magnify May with pockets full of posies.

Sleet slides in December sheets.
*Heaven has curled its yellow basket edges
just for you.* Arabian horses prance for you,

their tails sail. Near the fence the children dance,
posies in the sunset, and here are we three
nowhere, everywhere, ashes, ashes, world without end.

The Island of Black and White

All things turn, dreams in x-ray vision—
the shepherd's black sheep turns quickly white

when tossed over the fence on the Island of Black
and White. Light turns dark; dark,

light: shards of Celtic brio, liquid lies.
The grandfather I never knew,

whom one remembers swinging his daughters' arms
and belting "Let Me Call You Sweetheart,"

another recalls as a drunken Irish embarrassment
who gambled the family budget away.

Does it happen in other families, too,
views changing every generation

except for the one black sheep
who hops the fence once, turns color

but, for the rest of her life, regardless how many leaps
over how many fences, refuses to turn back?

Whale of a Dream

In this dream we sing
from wooden pews,
are shuffled to an airplane

safety drill which becomes
a cruise ship, the stained-
glass sanctuary now a vast

green sea with three
whales' tails suspended
fearsomely over water,

spray delayed mid-air.
No one else notices
we are rehearsing

for disaster as the blood-tale
spurts into spray
surrounding whale tails.

Yet the whales remain
in the sea, or become it
in sync, in spray.

More Water than Words

"I am poured out like water . . . ."
—Psalm 22:14

In sleep I'm back in my teenage lair,
old farmhouse's westward-facing bedroom—
hand-me-down Jenny Lind bed up against

a paneled, mouse-infested wall whose
scritch-scratching would keep me up when
pumpkin-sky melted into moonlight—

the room becomes a homely parlor where I join
cousin and sister to wring out the shirts
while it rains outside and in, water

tickles our ankles, soaks our socks,
wells up inside us, the dam bows
under pressure of enough water to require

reconstruction while, inside, outside,
clotheslines hold more shirts that
drip, drip. The weight of impending

loss watches us, washes us
as, together, we wring
and wring, nearly in unison,

little else to do until the sister
sets the laundry down to show
with upturned palm an array

of eyewear with rose or blue
lenses. She proffers them, urges me
to choose through which to look.

The Violist

Tending over, the waiting begins.
The musician enters gently, her hands
strong, her limbs long; her body

perfumes the air with peace.
She pulls bow from velvet box
which clatters to the floor. We laugh

the laugh of those with little choice. Beneath
the blanket the patient is present but
not, her breath a clanky motor; her eyes

flicker, sputter as if wired
to a switch so bad we don't know
if or when the walls will just erupt.

Viola hoisted, nestled chinward,
player lunges into one smooth strike
then another, then she twiddles knobs,

takes a long, deep breath, slowly
draws bow against the strings. We
hold our breath. Dvořák emerges

in splendor as mid-June swelters,
swaying. Patient's eyes blaze, her fingers
recall the feel of her own violin; her lips

tremble. We see her memory of stance
and bow. Aides linger at the door. Others
join. Every time her breathing rattles,

the violist plucks, pulls tendrils
of breath, first somber, soon rising
to a jig, each knee now a metronome.

The cat comes out of hiding,
curls, smiles. The stuck window
opens, her breath again

a gift like cicadas' punctual ecstasy.
Late spring modulates to C minor.
No one minds.

You Nibble Grilled Cheese

All moments now sacred, thoughts
can be touched. Eyes closing, you request
a grilled cheese sandwich at midnight

(I run home, fry it, hurry back)
and nibble it slowly, as sacrament.
Silence and talk mingle

like aesthetes at a gallery opening,
contented rivals who flit helplessly,
blinded by the lights they try to name.

Pound cake with red drizzle and white
foam cream. Sips of orange juice.
In your diminished shell I see the distant

woman who lit the sun with her own torch,
conversations, lives she entered, altered.
Mama, now your hands are trees.

Your eyes, skies too pained to speak,
grow soft as candlelight.

Synesthesia

How do you imagine what it's like to shed the flesh?
Is it the moment Michelangelo feels the sting

of fresco's eggy sludge cauterizing his eyes until
they see only with stamina of spirit?

Or the year Beethoven's world grows mute, yet
he hears a truer tune? I see Helen Keller

smile as she bursts brick walls
with a bellow because she perceives

with geyser force the heavy tongue
of water licking the palm of her hand

so every sinew springs up, and all her cells
require neither eyes nor voice to proclaim *I am.*

Damhsa

For your next number,
that tattered birthday suit

won't do. Go ahead. Take off
the bloated body,

let it fall with a sigh to the floor
as lightly soiled linen.

Meander through the Milky Way,
cavort with Cassiopoeia, brush

a comet's tail, ride the stamping bull,
rest on Saturn's rings.

Dance with the one you've pined for,
who won't take no for an answer.

Green and Burning Oak

Dair Glas Agus a Dhó
in memory of Eva Leah Robinson McCoy

So real it sears my hands, this
drawing, Celtic oak of two minds,
half-lobed and leafy, half-
smoke-and-flame-spewing,

muscular oak whose smoke
invokes and warns, whose
wood could hang Christ or
serve as his workshop lumber.

Crackling, unwithered, between
worlds, earth-rooted, limbs akimbo:
burl chars, sparks spiral,
ecstatically ablaze—

the way a human whose hand
has set her own body on fire
blurs the line between
bravery and madness—

the way you leave this world,
you, oak that, years ago, taking
earth and sun inside you, *dair
glas agus a dhó*, burned, churned out

us who loved you in your leaf-
green life. At the end your half-
fogged eyes blaze brightly, sky-
sparking as you lie drowning

while we sing to the tune
your voice used to chime out,
Be Thou my vision.
I rock you as you burn.

Keening

It comes back in a rush as you hold the one
who's at that border-bog between

greenness and fever-fire: your dream
where she stands tremulously then falls,

falls into you, heart to beating heart,
passes through your body, rises as a rush

of smoke toward the stained glass
high above your heads.

With nurse's hands now upon her wrist
comes the somber nod. A low horn howls

deep in distance yet grows nearer, red
and black and green, coyote call clawing

over many mountains in dim mist,
watery wail that worms its way

through, in a fit of frisson,
whatever beast you have become.

No Language for You

I cannot write about you yet. So I'm writing
about the lovely mess you left behind—
twisters, tears, silences

filled with all matter of clatter—
deadlines, loud movies, dramas—
not to mention stacks of clutter—

letters addressed, sealed, unsent;
boxes of papers you never opened;
tchotchkes, books, cards sent to you;

carved horses, glass horses; sacred texts
with newspaper clippings; notes to me scrawled
on angel cards and random slips of paper.

I know I have much more clutter of my own
with no deadline for its elimination. Rather,
I just don't know what day that is.

Dogwood, Oak, Birch

You walked beside me like pink dogwood—
now yours blooms and sways. Green
the lawn, the breeze, green the knitted

blanket for the never-born girl you show me
in bright dreams, green the tendrils that reach
past fields, gender, time—all now grand

and badly phrased illusions.
In the pine-paneled wall I see
your totem owl; inside closed eyes,

your deep brown eyes, bright face.
Your visage pops up everywhere.
You were the oak walking by my side,

who taught me to breathe words, open
lungs, pens, books, behold
in earth-encrusted bulbs, presence,

absence and the unity thereof,
the shadow's need for sun, sun's
acceptance of shadow as evidence of light.

We marveled at how uncertainty
holds our feet to ground; desire
tilts our faces toward the sun; one

insomniac mind finds another; stillness
tunes us in to chords pulsing all around.
A woman can walk on waves

if she doesn't gaze at the deep alone.
Yet in my chest a birch is breaking.
Outside all is howl, pelting. The cat

pushes paws into brown chenille
that was my mother's softest sweater.
Your laugh trickles into my ear just now.

Multilingual

At first you spoke only *tej*, the tongue
of milk, then of bread, *kênyer*, and soon,
new to walking, you came to words, *szóval*,

and books, *könyvek*, then *Krisztus* the babe,
Krisztus hanging, *Krisztus* the Good Shepherd.
At the age of six you taught your parents

hush for *hällgas*, *Come here* for *Gyere ide*
and all the other terms of parenting, early
learned the language of needle and thread

to appoint your husband's house with wildflowers
hímzett on linens, with carefully tufted
pillows of crimson *bársony*. You always spoke

rózafüzér when praying. When your boy wanted
a bike, you nudged him, smiling, toward his dad
for fathers spoke the tongue of *biciklis*.

You'd never scribed a recipe before your daughter-in-law
longed to roll the *töltött káposzta*; measuring ingredients
in handfuls, you penned the process, gleefully greeted

your granddaughter, read her *Winnie-az-Ugyan*,
placed those small hands in flour as they rolled the *kipfels*.
Even without *I love you*s, yours was the language of giving. Though words

had packed and gone by the time you cocooned, raising
a fist with one hand, blowing kisses with the other, at last you learned
the language of receiving, smiled for pressed hands, touched temple,

combed hair, straw-fed juice, crinkled eyes,
steadied rise, wiped flesh—offerings of *lámpa*,
the light surrounding everything.

Now, green world dissolved like snow, you dance the *csárdas*
with your man, then *Krisztus*, your feet conveying all you feel
in a language that needs no words.

Hy-Brasil

A big-hearted brainy broad born
to be a teacher went to bed last night
and never rose again, yet the sun
dares shine without her. Chocolate

turns to sand, to salt, to silt and still
the earth is green. Hands must
stroke the open wound to know
what's real—how Venus burns

brightly because sulphuric acid
reflects the rays of sun. How the isle
of Hy-Brasil knits an Aran mist
whose molecules have passed through

St. Brendan and Molly Brown alike.
How it disappears after five hundred years,
unuttered word at tongue's moist tip, then
rises from the sea, transmogrified

in fog and crystal skies. In dreams she still
wears streaks of summer in her hair,
inscribes notes of succor with a purple pen,
her smile wide as the ocean between us.

Letter to an Uninvited Guest

You crossed the sea to charm us all but strode in
tentatively. Uncertain whether introductions long ago
were sufficient to gain you entrance to our home,

you bore bouquets and compliments, vintage
merlot which we somehow feared to taste,
good books, good looks, good jokes, carrying

letters of introduction from every priest and rabbi in town.
You drew us out, drew us together, singing
hymns, spouting Shakespeare, Tolstoy, Tennyson.

You converse in any of a thousand tongues,
handsome in your good blue suit, despite a strange
choice for your lapel. But you've camped on our couch

for months. Your jokes have grown old, your teeth dark;
your crumpled suit reeks. You've stopped
trying to entertain us with anything

but your hypnotic eyes. You chomp
the end of a stale cigar I will not let you light;
you tap tobacco crumbs onto the floor.

You're not all bad, of course. You sit so still
for weeks that we scarcely notice you're
still here, but when we think of going out

you order in, then someone else goes out the door
feet first. Friends are dropping to the ground
like wing-clipped birds as you wanly smile.

Of course, we've thought of marching out without you,
Mr. D., but you've sworn you'll always follow.
How can you explain yourself?

You sing us softly to sleep with your Pavarotti voice.
The lily in your lapel smells sweeter now
than when you first arrived.

Play God

Someone died in the bedroom.
No one died in the bedroom. Someone
who lived there died, who radiated
life regardless of the tanks
and tubes. But that one is

gone now, not unmemorized, just harder
to reach by mental telegraph. Feel
compelled to paint the room a different
color, paint gray trim white and all the doors,
add a white fan on the ceiling, open

curtains to let the lilacs in. Think
of the back-yard birches—one of them
toppled in a storm, nearly taking out a room—
yet two remain. Stepping outside,
observe them, translate them

to canvas, a large canvas, for it must hold
a year of seasons, green, blue, orange,
purple. Vary each background, add
black spots to each birch. Still something's
missing. The trees lie flat as paper cut-outs,

background's greens, blues, oranges, purples
having all the fun. The scenes, though
invented, reveal themselves as false. This
will not do. Borrow a fine brush, mix
lapis, charcoal, heather, stroke each left side

with many lines, all the way to the root, then
add titanium, mix, and, with a lighter touch,
dab across and down each right side
again to the root. Take three steps back.
Trees' brightness seems credible at last: now

that they've emerged from white cocoons,
their grayness serves as a mantle of peace.
And so, at last, emerge
to know in your own trunk
the values of darkness, of light.

Midsummer Grief

Gray ionic clouds spin within as overhead
oak leaves whirl into a vortex higher than
neat shingled roofs. We want to be unpredictable yet
magnanimous-unafraid but mares and quarter horse

geldings gorgeous against green grub
snub extended hands as flies' blur menaces,
tails swish, eyes look at us askance.
Nearby many years ago freckled ten-year-olds

glimpsed in the mirror the jack-in-the-box girls who wore
our future faces. Now we black-worn women
unglass our eyes to recognize the gymnastic
swing of pathos' lurch toward helpfulness

in the elder's trembling hand, the pendulum time
of horsetails' swing. A green wind overtakes us.

Sitting Shiva in a Baptist Pew

Blessed be you, grinning, I'm sure, before your own
        urn, done at last with righteous pain's
        waves, crackles, stabs.

Blessed be you, heavy with horsehair and honeysuckle,
        full of bursts and booms and bounty,
        light with tales, embraces, lilting airs.

Blessed be the stacks of paper waiting
        for lines I don't know how to say
        and checks I cannot write.

Blessed be the lock that may or may not
        succeed in modulating
        the river's flood-force.

Blessed be the creaky door of peeled paint
        that opens slowly, shoots arrow-light
        toward those who keep eyes open.

Blessed be well-meaning friends who seem
        too cleanly to divide the yolks and whites
        of suffering and blessing.

Blessed be bagpipe, organ, poem, players, sayers
        who hear beyond background noise
        the music in the moment.

Blessed be the maple as it leans
        into a dipping sun that lights
        the torch of every leaf.

Blessed be the Spirit that defies definition,
    fear of every kind, all loud or
    whispered endings.

Blessed be these poor words I write
    in new combinations on the numb
    pages of my limbs.

Visitations

Whether fresh or familiar, grief comes oddly rushing.
We freeze the long winter through and think,
It's good to walk this ground again—I can't fall through,

it's rock, and yet at sun's first approach
that *rock* cascades in flood. So it is
to sit calmly, music playing: sudden

wafts of evergreen overwhelm, or, grasping
the doorknob, I sense a surge, and scent—
rose and rose with tinge of lilac—dons the air.

Might as well be a kerchief full of ether
the way it knocks me off my shoes.
Even smudges on the glass put on your face;

the blanket on my leg, your hand's caress.
The forgotten angel card you sent me years ago
wings softly to my feet just before

phones' ringing signals yet another death.
The basket of notes you penned in dwindling days
overflows, leaving in your wake

a room without a use,
an empty pen, a singer
who's forgotten the song.

The Question

When we've gathered to bury your ashes at last
you give me the world in a dream.
White laboratory. Women in white bearing beakers.

I ask them the purpose of their experiments
but no one speaks my language.
One points me toward an adjacent room

whose white door is shut. I enter. There
you are, in the silk you wore at my wedding,
gazing at me in your pink dress,

hair dark, legs slender columns once again.
Your crisp features dissolve like yeast. Now
your face morphs: in your space a tall black woman

who knows a wholly different life, red cardigan,
white pocketbook hooked on her arm. Now you turn
into a short white man, now a native, spinning

ever faster—person after person shares
a history and atomic space where your body was.
Beaming in silence you give it to me straight,

the answer I asked for before you died,
whether we are sentenced or graced
to death and life and death and life again.

What if Genesis' creation story repeats for reason,
the word, the long labor of a pregnant woman who
crouches to birth herself?

The Wheel

In a few billion years—weeks to heaven—
the sun becomes a red giant, dying star
destined for eventual rebirth

on the other side of the great black
hole at the center of our galaxy.
The sun flares even now

the way Isadora Duncan's red scarf trails,
catches in the turning tire,
chokes her. The wheel keeps turning,

chrome flashes in the sun, and we can only
wonder whether Isadora wakes to live another day
wearing someone else's life.

Rooms in Mourning

Robed in fog, shuffle coffeeward,
batting at sticky, invisible webs
of dreams that seemed important
but melt like sugar in your cup.

Outside, a morning sparrow swoops,
lands, pauses, facing the window,
tiny eyes alert. She's nested
in the eaves. Temper your sense

of encroachment with a dab of wonder
at all your old house can contain
as sparrow's grayish feathers
light up in morning sun. Recall

when your room emptied, notice
as other rooms darken. Swallow turns,
rises, flaps back to the nest. In such small
gray space, tough twigs interwoven

with silken threads of grass,
marvels happen. Mouths open,
are filled, cry, are filled again, sing.
Sunlight, moonlight enter in equal measure.

Each time the mama leaves, fledglings'
world ends. Back in she swoops, bearing
luscious grubs, berries. She sings morning,
knows the fall precedes the flight.

Waken before the coffee hits your lips.

Rise

I don't know their name,
translucent crisscrossed fingers of light
that appear between families

of clouds: they aren't
cirrus, nor cumulonimbus,
nor mere wisps; they have

body and angle and sheerness.
Their geometry's precise.
They don't care what glorious

loops of cloud surround them,
nor do they vanish in heat of day.
They roll on without seeming

to move at all; they rise
without yielding; they let you
see through them if

you'll bother to look.
They are the quotidian gases
between layers of beauty and dust.

They proclaim their identity
and claim their space
in stillness.

They breathe together,
neither wholly separate nor
merged into a pool of cloudiness.

Around them, horse herds gallop past,
spirits of trees and natives hold court, yet,
plumply incorporeal, they rise, real.

Light filters through them
in the space between this world
and the rest.

Notes

"Through a Glass, Darkly"
"For now we see through a glass, darkly; but then face to face: now I know in part; but then shall I know even as also I am known."--I Corinthians 13:12, King James Version.

"The Island of Black and White"
This is an island of Celtic myth in the voyage to the Otherworld in which a sheep will change color when tossed over the fence, suggesting how we each "change color" when stripped of a familiar environment, or of our own egos.

"Damhsa"
Damhsa (dow-suh) is the Irish word for "dance." Cassiopeia is both a constellation and, in Greek mythology, the wife of King Cepheus of Ethiopia, a woman whose boasting angered Poseidon. She sacrificed her daughter Andromeda to the sea to appease the sea god, but Andromeda was rescued by Perseus, who married her. "Dance with the one you've pined for / who won't take no for an answer" alludes to the poem "I Won't Take No for an Answer" by the fourteenth century Italian St. Catherine of Siena.

"Green and Burning Oak"
According to *The Celtic Book of the Dead* by Caitlin Matthews, "This is one of the primal images of the Otherworld in British Celtic tradition. To encounter it signifies the change from one mode of being to another. . . ." Celtic lore and contemporary artists depict a giant oak, half bursting with green leaves, half aflame, to signify this state of being rife with danger, enticement, mystery. The Irish Gaelic phrase "*dair glas agus a dhó*" may be translated as "green and burning oak." Regarding "Be Thou My Vision," according to the Discipleship Ministries of the United Methodist Church website, "The Irish text, beginning '*Rob tu mo bhoile, a Comdi cride*,' was translated into literal prose by Irish scholar Mary Byrne (1880-1931), a Dublin native, and then published in *Eriú*, the journal of the School of Irish Learning, in 1905." Irish liturgical

scholar Helen Phelan emphasizes that the heroic imagery for God in the Irish text depicts God as a high chieftain who protects his people, a technique typical of medieval Irish poetry.

"Multilingual"
The terms in this elegy for my mother-in-law are Hungarian. *Tej,* tongue; *kênyer,* bread; *szóval,* words; *könyvek,* books; *Krisztus,* Christ; *hímzett,* embroidered; *bársony,* velvet; *rózafüzér,* rosary; *biciklis,* bicycles; *töltött káposzta,* stuffed cabbage; *Winnie-az-Ugyan,* Winnie-the-Pooh; *kipfels,* filled, rolled cookies eaten at Christmas and Easter; *lámpa,* light; *csárdas,* lively traditional Hungarian folk dance.

"Hy-Brasil"
The title refers to a mythical island said to rise periodically from the foggy Atlantic off the west coast of Ireland and disappear again.

Additional Acknowledgments

The poems in this chapbook were written in memory or in honor of the following persons: "Through a Glass, Darkly" honors Pauline McCoy Koran; "Textures" honors Alva Pennington McCoy; "More Water Than Words" honors Christine McCoy Bruner and Pamela Ann Aronoff Minor and memorializes Patsy Ann Robinson Aronoff and Eva Leah Robinson McCoy; "The Violist" honors Dr. Lale Davidson; "Dogwood, Oak, Birch" was written in memory of Dr. Gwen Cranfill Curry for Marcie Sloan McGuire; "Multilingual," in memory of Catherine Nadenichek Medve; "Hy-Brasil," in memory of Carole Dunson Moreau; "Midsummer Grief," in memory of Gordon Aronoff, Jr. and in honor of Karen, Jessica, and Nicole Aronoff. All other poems in this volume were written in memory of Eva Leah Robinson McCoy.

I am particularly grateful to Leah Maines, who selected this manuscript; Christen Kincaid, my editor; Kevin Maines, Elizabeth Maines, and the staff of Finishing Line Press; Marilyn McCabe who read the draft of this manuscript, and the other Women of Mass Dissemination--Dr. Lale Davidson, Nancy White, Dr. Elaine Handley, and Mary Sanders Shartle, for their wise-woman creativity and support (see womenofmassdissemination.wordpress.com), and Barbara Hall and Karen Squires who helped care for Eva in her final years. Special love to Bob and Elizabeth Medve, Christine McCoy Bruner, Rev. Linda Hoeschle, and all of my family, especially Bill and Alva McCoy.

www.ingramcontent.com/pod-product-compliance
Lightning Source LLC
LaVergne TN
LVHW051609080426
835510LV00020B/3199